DRD4
The Connections

T.R. Lewis

ISBN: 153038141X
ISBN-13: 978-1530381418

DEDICATION

I have to dedicate this book to all of the deranged people either in my life or who have touched my life in some way. I've had the pleasure to grow up in a non-traditional lifestyle and that has permitted me to be exposed to many different types of people as well as many different scenarios that many couldn't phantom.

CONTENTS

Contents

ACKNOWLEDGMENTS

I have to give thanks to all of the many people that have crossed my path and in doing so have in one form or another contributed to my knowledge and experience that helped construct my beliefs as well as research into this book.

This book is the work of many years of interaction with liberals, mentally challenged, drug addicts and alcoholics without them this would book would be just speculation and have no merit, with them this book becomes hope that it is possible to live and be a productive member of society.

I've also used many different research avenues all of which I have added references to in the endnotes section of this book. There are too many sources to list in this section.

So thank you society for all of the entertainment and knowledge you have so graciously given to me for use in my quest.

Why I Wrote This Book

That's an easy answer, well kind of anyways. It's no surprise that I am an independent conservative, mainly because I have a brain that can rationalize and I'm capable of doing my own research, unlike most liberals.

Throughout life I've always questioned things and I have always dug deeply for answers that others wouldn't even see the questions too. The fact that I was known as the "what-if kid" in school was no coincidence that I grew up to be who I am now.

Now I am, for those who don't know, a person who says things how they are and I don't really give a crap as to whether or not you like what I have to say. Yes, I've learned to put filters in place from time to time but only where absolutely necessary and only when absolutely necessary. But I will never end up being a good sales person or good in a corporate environment unless I am at the top of the food chain because kissing ass is not a strong suit of mine and I have absolutely no respect for those that run around with a brown nose.

Sales people for the most part are predominantly liberal and have no problem convincing the prospect (sucker, mark, conned) into believing that they cannot live without whatever product they are selling today. They end up building really strong relationships and a sort of following that they can continue to manipulate the thoughts into what it is that is needed for the current situation.

Now it may sound like I am picking on sales people but

that is not the case, fact is drug, addicts, alcoholics and con men are the same. Why is that and why does it continue to happen throughout their lives is the bigger question and one that is fairly easy to explain.

In this book I will take a look at the DRD4 gene and my theories as to how it applies to these conditions based on research and my personal information gathering from many people with the genetic defect. I will focus more on sales people and addicts but will touch base on liberals as well because, again, most sales people and addicts are also liberals.

DRD4 Quick Breakdown

Below is the scientific explanations of the DRD4 and what it does and doesn't do. Then we will go into the actual defects and how the a genetic defect will effect different people. You will get to dive into the actual scientific world of the functions and learn more then you need to and that's because I wouldn't be doing justice without having all of the information here.

The dopamine receptor D4 is a G protein-coupled receptor encoded by the DRD4 gene.[i] As with other dopamine receptor subtypes, the D4 receptor is activated by the neurotransmitter dopamine. It is linked to many neurological and psychiatric conditions[ii] including schizophrenia and bipolar disorder,[iii] addictive behaviors,[iv] Parkinson's disease,[v] and eating disorders such as anorexia nervosa.[vi]

It is also a target for drugs which treat schizophrenia and Parkinson disease.[vii] The D4 receptor is considered to be D2-like in which the activated receptor inhibits the enzyme adenylate cyclase, thereby reducing the intracellular concentration of the second messenger cyclic AMP. [viii]

Genetics

The human protein is coded by the DRD4 on chromosome 11 located in 11p15.5.

There are slight variations (mutations/polymorphisms) in the human gene:

- A 48-base pair VNTR in exon 3
- C-521T in the promoter
- 13-base pair deletion of bases 235 to 247 in exon 1
- 12 base pair repeat in exon 1.[ix]
- Val194Gly

A polymorphic tandem duplication of 120 bp

Mutations in this gene have been associated with various behavioral phenotypes, including autonomic nervous system dysfunction, attention deficit/hyperactivity disorder,[x] schizophrenia,[xi] and the personality trait of novelty seeking.[xii]

48-Base Pair VNTR

The 48-base pair VNTR in exon 3 range from 2 to 11 repeats.

DRD4-7R, the 7-repeat (7R) variant of DRD4, has been linked to a susceptibility for developing ADHD in several meta-analyses and other psychological traits and disorders.[xiii] [xiv]

The frequency of the alleles varies greatly between populations, e.g., the 7-repeat version has high incidence in America and low in Asia.[xv] "Long" versions of polymorphisms are the alleles with 6 to 10 repeats. 7R appears to react less strongly to dopamine molecules.[xvi]

The 48-base pair VNTR has been the subject of much speculation about its evolution and role in human behaviors cross-culturally. The 7R allele appears to have been selected for about 40,000 years ago. [xvii] In 1999 Chen and colleagues[xviii] observed that populations who migrated farther in the past 30,000 to 1,000 years ago had a higher frequency of 7R/long alleles. They also showed that nomadic populations had higher frequencies of 7R alleles than sedentary ones. More recently it was observed that the health status of nomadic Ariaal men was higher if they had 7R alleles. However, in recently sedentary (non-nomadic) Ariaal those with 7R alleles seemed to have slightly deteriorated health.[xix]

Novelty (Thrill) Seeking

Despite early findings of an association between the DRD4 48bp VNTR and novelty seeking (a characteristic of exploratory and excitable people), The meta-analysis of 11 studies did find that another polymorphism in the gene, the -521C/T, showed an association with novelty seeking.[xx] In our beliefs based on those factors, novelty-seeking behavior is attributable to DRD4 and continues to help drive the behaviors for the adults as well as the children affected by the defect.

This is important because there seems to be a direct correlation between addicts, LGBT and liberals where the genetic defect is detected, by giving the subject a sense of not wanting to be in reality but rather they constantly seek the self-generated reality where they are safe, protected and rewarded constantly.

This behavior seems to drive the addict to the point that combined with other behaviors makes true reality unbearable to them to the point that without something to suppress reality in their system they can't function correctly in what should be normal situations.

Cognitive Development

Several studies have suggested that parenting may affect the cognitive development of children with the 7-repeat allele of DRD4.[xxi] Parenting that has maternal sensitivity, mindfulness, and autonomy–support at 15 months was found to alter children's executive functions at 18 to 20 months. [xxii] Children with poorer quality parenting were more impulsive and sensation seeking than those with higher quality parenting. [xxiii] Higher quality parenting was associated with better effortful control in 4-year-olds. [xxiv]

The quick breakdown here is that without the quality parenting at the right time of development then the subject is more likely to be impulsive as well as looking for that feel good moment leading to the subject to essentially caring only about oneself and their own rewards at any cost.

Ligands

Chemical structures of representative D4-preferring ligands.

Agonists[edit]

WAY-100635: potent full agonist, with 5-HT1A antagonistic component[xxv]

A-412,997: full agonist, > 100-fold selective over a panel of seventy different receptors and ion channels[xxvi]

ABT-724 - developed for treatment of erectile dysfunction[xxvii]

ABT-670 - better oral bioavailability than ABT-724[xxviii]

FAUC 316: partial agonist, > 8600-fold selective over other dopamine receptor subtypes[xxix]

FAUC 299: partial agonist[xxx]

(E)-1-aryl-3-(4-pyridinepiperazin-1-yl)propanone oximes[xxxi]

PIP3EA: partial agonist[xxxii]

Flibanserin - partial agonist

PD-168,077 - D4 selective but also binds to α1A, α2C and 5HT1A

CP-226,269 - D4 selective but also binds to D2, D3, α2A, α2C and 5HT1A

Ro10-5824 - partial agonist

Roxindole (also D2 and D3 autoreceptor partial agonist, 5HT1A receptor agonist, serotonin reuptake inhibitor)pomorphine also adrenergic and 5ht agonist, most affinity for the D4 subtype

Antagonists

A-381393: potent, subtype selective antagonist (>2700-fold)[xxxiii]

FAUC 213[xxxiv]

L-745,870[xxxv] [xxxvi]

L-750,667[xxxvii]

S 18126: also σ1 affin[xxxviii]

Fananserin - mixed 5-HT2A / D4 antagonist

Clozapine, an atypical antipsychotic

Buspirone, an anxiolytic

Inverse Agonists

FAUC F41: inverse agonist, subtype selectivity of more than 3 orders of magnitude over D2 and D3[xxxix xl]

A Little Background On DRD4

Ebstein[xli] first highlighted the drama of an 'adventure gene': the dopamine D4 receptor gene (DRD4) and its association with substance abuse and personality. This was followed with a report by Baron[xlii] who suggested that this drama is sagging due to conflicting reports emerging. It now appears that the drama continues with 'severity of dependence' to substance abuse, another variable that may be pertinent to the DRD4 association.[xliii]

In 1996, Ebstein and colleagues[xliv] examined DRD4 and its association with the human personality trait Novelty Seeking (NS) in a sample of healthy volunteers recruited from an unrelated. Israeli staff/student population. Using Cloninger's Tridimensional Personality Questionnaire (TPQ)[xlv] to measure NS (high novelty seekers are characterized by their impulsive and exploratory behavior), they reported an association between the DRD4 gene and normal human personality. They analyzed TPQ scores and frequency of DRD4 exon III repeat polymorphisms in 124 samples and found that subjects with the seven-repeat allele exhibited significantly higher NS scores when compared to subjects lacking the seven-repeat allele. This association did not appear to be due to population stratification as it was independent of ethnicity, age or sex of the subjects (69 men, 55 women, mean age 29.8 years).

Benjamin et al[xlvi] provided support for this initial study by investigating the relationship between the DRD4 exon III sequence variant and personality test scores amongst a sample of 315 American family members and individuals. The study confirmed initial findings of the Ebstein et al study[xlvii] despite methodological differences. For example, Benjamin et al used a sample of white Americans, of whom 95% were male. In addition, they employed Eysenck's NEO-PI-R, which is based upon a trait model of personality, with NS falling in the extraversion factor. This is in contrast to the TPQ, which is based on a biological model in which three independent dimensions of temperament are attributed to genetically and neurochemically distinct pathways, with novelty seeking being mediated by dopamine neurotransmission.[xlviii] Finally, Benjamin et al6 did not examine presence or absence of the seven-repeat allele, but grouped individual genotypes into long or short alleles on the gene. Subjects with the long alleles were found to be significantly higher novelty seekers than those with the short alleles.

A third study, conducted by Ebstein[xlix] offered additional evidence for the association with DRD4 and NS, using similar methods to their previous study. In the same year, Ono and colleagues[l] conducted a similar study with 153 normal, Japanese women (mean age 18.7 years). They used the TPQ to measure NS and found an association with long alleles at the polymorphic exon III repeats sequence of DRD4 and NS.

Evidence continued to build for the association between DRD4 and NS amongst healthy people with different ethnic origins. To date, a further six studies[li],[lii],[liii],[liv],[lv],[lvi] have been published, making a total of ten studies offering support for this association. One study used a sample of 119, twelve-year-old Caucasian boys,[lvii] there have been two Japanese studies,10,12 a Finnish study,[lviii] an Israeli study[lix] and a German study[lx] conducted.

Despite substantial evidence emerging for the association between the DRD4 gene variant and NS, there have been only a few conflicting reports showing a lack of association between these variables[lxi,lxii,lxiii,lxiv,lxv,lxvi,lxvii,lxviii,lxix,lxx] which may be attributable to basic methodological differences between studies. Ebstein[lxxi] established guidelines for conducting such research and in doing so highlighted the controversy surrounding this association. Baron[lxxii] swiftly responded by offering constructive criticism concerning methodological issues surrounding this research, questioning whether the drama of the 'adventure gene'.

Research refuting the association with DRD4 and NS began in 1996 [lxxiii] and was shortly followed by three articles in 1997 [lxxiv,lxxv,lxxvi] four articles in 1998 [lxxvii,lxxviii,lxxix,lxxx] and two in 1999 [lxxxi,lxxxii] There are several possible reasons as to why these studies failed to find an association with DRD4 and NS. Firstly, age is an important variable to consider in personality research. NS diminishes with age so to obtain consistent personality scores, subjects should be young (ideally under the age of 45 years)[lxxxiii] Reports providing evidence for the association with DRD4 and NS used subjects between the ages of 12-35 years.[lxxxiv,lxxxv,lxxxvi,lxxxvii,lxxxviii,lxxxix,xc,xci,xcii,xciii] The subjects used in studies that failed to find a significant association with DRD4 and NS were older, between 18-62 years.[xciv,xcv,xcvi,xcvii,xcviii,xcix,c,ci,cii,ciii] Of these studies reporting negative findings, 60% employed subjects who were over the age of 35 years.[civ,cv,cvi,cvii,cviii,cix] It appears that negative results may have been obtained because NS levels were lower in these people because they were older.

Secondly, failure to find an association with DRD4 and NS may be due to the lack of uniformity actually employed when measuring the personality trait. Scales with high retest reliability and valid for use with a variety of populations and cultures should be used for this research.[cx] The TPQ Novelty Seeking scale and the ZKPQ Sensation Seeking Scale are suitable and moderately correlated allowing results to be generalized across different studies.[cxi] Failure to find associations with DRD4 and personality traits may be due to authors using different personality scales to measure NS.

Another factor that may be pertinent to the association is ethnicity. So far, studies have used Israeli, Japanese, American, Swedish, Finnish and German populations. The association may be dependent upon ethnicity as genetic variants vary across different ethnic groups. It is highly possible as well as plausible that the relationship between DRD4 and NS is real, but only in some populations and not others.

Gender is another variable to be considered in light of these conflicting findings. Mixed gender groups of sufficient size should be used for this research. A good example, the Japanese replication study observing an association was restricted to women.[cxii] Whereas the Finnish study which did not observe a significant association with DRD4 and NS only included men.[cxiii] This controversy may have been due to different gender groups being used in each study.

While the search for a true association with DRD4 and NS continues, the search for genes associated with substance abuse is taking the same theme. Similar conflicting findings are also reported in substance abuse with half of the studies reporting a significant association with the DRD4 gene variant[cxiv, cxv, cxvi, cxvii, cxviii, cxix] whilst the other half have failed to replicate this association.[cxx],[cxxi],[cxxii],[cxxiii],[cxxiv],[cxxv],[cxxvi],[cxxvii]

The pattern that is emerging is that significant associations between DRD4 and substance abuse are found amongst samples of drug abusers (heroin and nicotine dependence)[cxxviii],[cxxix],[cxxx] and non-significant results are yielded from samples of alcohol abusers. [cxxxi],[cxxxii],[cxxxiii],[cxxxiv],[cxxxv],[cxxxvi],[cxxxvii]One study did find a significant association with DRD4 and alcohol abuse but this was only observed in alcohol abusers who were distinguished by the ALDH2 polymorphism.[cxxxviii] ALDH22 (as opposed to ALDH21) is an allele whose presence causes a flushing reaction following alcohol ingestion which therefore acts protectively to lower the incidence of alcoholism in people with this genotype.

Furthermore, diagnosing substance abuse may be another important factor that may influence the results obtained from these association studies. If substance abuse or dependence status is not clearly defined amongst the sample or controls, then associations between variables may not be found due to the substance abuse group being too similar to the control group. This issue gives rise to the continuation of the drama with the association between DRD4, substance abuse and NS. A recent study[cxxxix] measured severity of dependence and failed to support previous findings of a significant association with DRD4 and substance abuse. However, results did suggest that possession of the long-repeat genotype at the DRD4 receptor makes an individual more susceptible to severe dependence upon a substance. This study indicated that substance-dependent subjects who possess the long-repeat genotype rate their severity of dependence significantly higher than those with the short-repeat genotype. It was concluded from this study that the variant at DRD4 does not increase susceptibility to dependence per se, but that the variant may partially determine severity of dependence.[cxl] The lack of association previously reported might have occurred because dependence severity was not analyzed in association with genotype.

To highlight the importance of dependence severity in association studies another study has since reported an association between pathological gambling and the Monoamine Oxidase gene (MAOA) polymorphism.[cxli] The study found no significant differences between pathological gamblers and healthy controls in overall allele distribution at the MAOA gene but when severity of gambling was considered they did find a significant association between allele distribution in a subgroup of severe gamblers.

By reviewing this recent research, it can be concluded that there may be an association with DRD4 and NS amongst severe drug-dependent populations. Therefore, the DRD4 gene may not predispose individuals to addiction per se, but having the genetic variant may predispose substance abusers to a severe dependency. Therefore, does the drama continue for the DRD4 gene and its association with NS and substance abuse?

Problems with Current Belief

We've all have known that women are the hardest creature to understand and with very good reasoning as it would seem. We've spent years trying to understand women and this might just be a little bit of an insight for men or might not at all.

There is also the fact that a generally large population of the LGBT community are very liberal as well as being more promiscuous then the average person and throw in the fact that there is currently an extremely high rate of addiction issues within the LGBT community.

Or, to be precise, a specific variant of one gene that would seem to exert greater sway over women, LGBT community than straight men.

Working with 1771 university students of Han Chinese origin in Singapore, researchers compared answers to surveys, including one tailored to hot-button issues in the city-state, with the presence of a permutation of the DRD4 gene.

DRD4 is one of several genes that determines the way dopamine, a crucial neurotransmitter, or chemical messenger, is released in the brain. Dopamine is the chemical that gives the brain the feel good responses to things that it likes.

What they found was a definite link between the presence (or not) of the variant and a split between liberals inclined to decry inequality, racism and other off the wall canned responses to anyone who gets in their way of feeling good for a made up cause, on the one hand, and die-hard conservative wary of change, on the other.

"The association between political attitude and DRD4 was highly significant for females," and while still there, less so for men, said the study, led by Richard Ebstein of the National University of Singapore.

Women without the defect, it was also shown, tended to be more conservative in general.

The results are elevated by earlier research based on people of European descent that found similar patterns around the same gene, according to the study.

In the long-standing "Nature vs. Nurture" debate, it was long assumed that social values—and especially political ones—were rooted in family upbringing, education and class.

But a growing pile of evidence suggests, in the words of the researchers, that "biology can't continue to be ignored."

A landmark study published in 1999, for example, of twins separated at or near birth showed a marked strain of heritability for 'conservatism'.

The brain is wired with several distinct dopamine pathways, including one related to the risk-taking—arguably a parallel to the liberal-conservative dichotomy.

From an evolutionary standpoint, risk-taking is a

complicated as all hell: in some situations, it may enhance one's chances of success or survival, and in others it may end an entire species.

In the study, the researchers used standard questionnaires to rate conservative or liberal tendencies, making it easier to compare with earlier efforts to uncover links between genes and attitudes.

At the same time, to adjust for cultural variations from one country to another, they also devised a survey based on local issues known to divide opinion in Singapore along political lines.

One set of questions, for example, asked the students, half men, half women with a mean age of 21, to take positions on sensitive environmental and animal rights issues.

The correlation with the genetic variations was especially strong on these points.

"Our results provide evidence," Ebstein and colleagues conclude, "for a role of the DRD4 gene variants in contributing to individual differences"

The Real Problem of Current Beliefs

If you look at all the research you will see there is a common theme going on here, the theme is liberals control these colleges as well as most of these studies in one way or another, including scientist payroll, so it's not surprising that they try to lean the data to make them look better. When you look at the facts and look at them with a non-judgmental outlook and apply a little bit of history and self-experience coupled with commonsense to the equation you will see that my beliefs are correct or at the very least highly plausible.

Once the standard becomes in line with the correct beliefs then this will permit society to better understand what the devastating effects are and possible lead to treatment or rehabilitation possibilities that can permit these people to actually live productive lives in much the same way as any other person may.

It's no secret that there are many who suffer from the DRD4 genetic defect and still live productive lives for the most part. If we learn how they do it and what was key to their success then we will be one step closer to the development of an outline on how to raise children with the defect as well as how to treat adults with the defect.

Novity (Thrill Seeking)

In what is being called a first of its kind study (Like we couldn't of told them this), researchers at Binghamton University, State University of New York (SUNY) have discovered that about half of all people have a gene that makes them more vulnerable to promiscuity and cheating.

Those with a certain variant of the dopamine receptor D4 polymorphism -- or DRD4 gene -- "were more likely to have a history of uncommitted sex, including one-night stands and acts of infidelity," according to lead investigator Justin Garcia.

DRD4 is the "thrill-seeking" gene, also responsible for alcohol and gambling addictions. The gene can influence the brain's chemistry and subsequently, an individual's behavior.

The desire to cheat or sleep around seems to originate in the brain's pleasure and reward center, where the "rush" of dopamine motivates those who are vulnerable, the researchers say.

In the study, Garcia instructed 181 student volunteers at SUNY to take an anonymous survey on their previous sexual behavior, asking them questions like how many sex partners they had and if they had ever been unfaithful.

He then tested their DNA by oral rinsing with a special mouthwash -- a buccal wash -- and genotyped the DRD4.

His team discovered that there is a variation in the thrill-seeking gene and those with much longer alleles are more prone to, well, getting prone. (An allele is part of the gene's DNA sequence responsible for different traits such as eye color or curly hair.)

Those with at least one 7-repeat allele reported a higher rate of promiscuity -- that is admitting to a "one-night stand." The same group had a 50 percent increase in instances of sexual cheating.

"It turns out everyone has got the gene," said Garcia, who is a doctoral fellow in the laboratory of evolutionary anthropology and health at SUNY Binghamton. "Just as height varies, the amount of information in the gene varies. In those who have more, their alleles are longer and they are more prone to thrill-seeking."

"It's inheritable, too," he said. "If your parents have it, you have it." This not good for the future of liberals unless they either stop breeding or learn to treat those with the genetic defect at an early age.

When the brain is stimulated -- drinking alcohol, jumping from planes, having sex -- it releases dopamine, the pleasure response hormone.

"It's rewarding and makes us excited and gives us pleasure," said Garcia. "But the people with the DRD4 gene need more stimuli to feel satiated. Some of say 'wow,' that was a rush after jumping out of a plane. Others ask, 'When is the plane going back up?'" the same holds true for liberals and addicts alike.

But not all are convinced a roaming eye is rooted in DNA.

"Certain people are vulnerable to affairs, but in the end, it's about personal choice," said Jenn Berman, a psychotherapist and host of "The Love and Sex Show" on Cosmo Radio. "And it depends on how well-developed their impulse control is.", the muscle to suppress can be built up and take control over the mind.

Still, the study could have some interesting implications.

Armed with that kind of data, John Coleman said he might be inclined to test his fiancé and himself as well.

"It's like getting tested for STDs," he said. "It's the ultimate form of honesty, really," he said obviously not trusting his fiancé.

But Garcia said the gene for risk also might have an evolutionary advantage, beyond producing more children.

The gene evolved about 30,000 to 50,000 years ago when humans were moving out of Africa.

"Having some individuals who have wanderlust and want to see what's on the other side mountain. It's important for new places to live. But it's also risk-taking. Sometimes, going to the other side of the mountain means that something eats you. There is a cost and a benefit." Those with the genetic defect don't care about nothing but the immediate rush others that do the exploring are actually doing it for mankind.

Some of the implications of this study might be "huge," and not just in the bedroom. "The big question is what happens in drug rehab if you have a long allele and others don't? They might have different treatments." And if not recognized early enough there might only be slim chance of a successful treatment.

Once the behavior has taken control and priority over every core thought and instinct to the point that all of your self-proclaimed role models are addicts and cheaters that just so happened to live a somewhat successful life, no matter the cost they've taxed on to others with to do so and no matter what moral character they've had to dismiss, if these are the role models that are being sought out then it's safe to say that the genetic defect has taken hold an rooted in deep. Without the true desire to overcome it being a full driving force then chances are severely reduced of ever overcoming the defect.

Not All Who Have Gene Will Be Sluts or Cheaters or Drug Addicts or Liberals

The study also strongly suggests that sex drive and thrill can function independently of love. This is also present even in couples that love each other and plays out as one or both having an unreasonable drive of lust with the one that they actual love and defining sex as the main definition of being together.

That might be the case with Emma, a 20-year-old student from University of Southern Florida, who just broken up with her boyfriend after a two-year monogamous relationship.

She wanted to try something different, so she slept with three men in one month. Two were encounters with guys she had been friends with and another was a fling that transformed into a longer relationship.

"I'd never done anything like that before," said Emma, who did not want to reveal her last name. "It was something so new to me."

She said it's not in her personality to take risks. Defying college stereotypes, Emma's never touched alcohol and has only smoked marijuana once.

And now that she is in a committed relationship, Emma is certain she won't be unfaithful.

Upbringing, experience and culture may actually wield more influence than the risk-taking gene, according to

Susan Quilliam, a noted British psychologist and author of the updated "Joy of Sex."

"We are learning more and more about genes implicated in behaviors," she said. "Every time a genetic study comes out, responsible scientists also stress that we have choice -- nature and nurture," she said. Knowing that the choice was second to the impulse.

"Not everyone with the gene is promiscuous and not everyone who is promiscuous will have that gene." But the fact remains that you're more likely to be promiscuous if you have the gene.

And Can't Risk-Taking Be a Good Thing?

"Sometimes that overlaps with creativity, with entrepreneurship and wanting to push the boundaries," she said. "In relationships that can be exciting and fulfilling and help the whole couple move into new areas."

So should a woman have her boyfriend tested before accepting his marriage proposal?

"By the time she meets him, unless he is very young, his track record will prove whether he has acted on his infidelity gene or not," said Quilliam. "If he has been unfaithful in the past, he is likely to do it in the future."

Maureen Finn, a 19-year-old television, film and radio major at Syracuse University, agrees.

"I mean if you meet a guy at a party and he's making out with three other girls, that's a hint," she said. "If you're disrespecting me, something tells me you're not going to respect me enough to be faithful."

Drug Addicts as well as other Addicts

When you look at addicts and their core beliefs you will see a lot of commonalities, together with liberals the common drive for both of these groups are simple. To simple really for others being paid millions and getting billions in funding to document and continue getting their funds.

Let's look at what we have learned from the DRD4 so far and apply some common sense.

1) Novelty(Thrill) Seeking – In psychology, novelty seeking (NS) is a personality trait associated with exploratory activity in response to novel stimulation, impulsive decision making, extravagance in approach to reward cues, and quick loss of temper and avoidance of frustration.
    a. Exploratory activity in response to novel stimulation.

    Doing something that makes you feel good, even if the activity is new and or dangerous in nature. As long as they get the FEEL GOOD moment or the chance of the feel good moment, then they are good with it.

    b. Impulsive decision making.

    Deciding to do something without thinking it through, usually for end up with the FEEL GOOD moment, or the chance of the feel good moment, then they are good with it mentioned above.

c. Extravagance in approach to reward cues

Extravagance is defined as Extreme; wild; excessive; unrestrained, so it's easy to see where this leads to, they will do anything for the reward FEEL GOOD moment., or the chance of the feel good moment, then they are good with it.

d. Quick loss of temper.

Since anything that gets in the way of the FEEL GOOD moment can be considered as hostile then to them they are justified in defending any means to the FEEL GOOD moment without thought or with very little thought,

e. Avoidance of frustration.

It's easy to explain this one, if one isn't in the FEEL GOOD moment then they are frustrated and that adds to the motivation to get back to the FEEL GOOD moment, or the chance of the feel good moment, then they are good with it.

2) Cognitive Development

This doesn't need so much breaking down as the previous however plays an important role in addiction. Because of this addicts are more impulsive and sensation seeking than others, a product that has grown from childhood

Now with these two genetically altered factors and no intervention at early childhood to help teach the correct behaviors then there really isn't a chance is there?

I'm not blaming parents, what I am saying is that from an early stage in life and usually re-enforced throughout life (from the FEEL GOOD moments) then the brain has only one way to develop and like a muscle it gets stronger in that response and makes other responses even harder.

Does that mean there is no hope for an addict with DRD4, of course not, as most mental deficiencies they can be taught how to cope with the current situation and develop other rewards that provide the dopamine for the FEEL GOOD moment.

This isn't something that happens overnight and usually can't happen unless the addict actually is willing, remember these same genetic defects makes it a natural response to lie, cheat and manipulate to get to the FEEL GOOD moment that they are used too. That includes danger, without thought and with a tremendous driving force that seems to consume their consciousness.

Those that had started feeding into the addiction and negative behavior at a younger ager have missed the normal development stages of their brain and therefor aren't equipped mentally to handle things that others can manage without thought, remember they've never flexed those muscles at all.

Without the FEEL GOOD moment and still with the DRD4 genetic defect permitting the brain to take control to feed into the DRD4 requests, one will have a long path to sobriety. It will take motivation and will power that the addict has only used to feed the desires of the defect to consciously be focused on defeating the defect at hand.

Liberal's

The exact behavior can be attributed to a liberals and their actions as to the addicts mentioned before. The main issue here is that this behavior doesn't just effect their lives but actual communities as well as countries and entire species are at risk and therefore this needs to be monitored and intercepted as soon as possible.

Take for instance the liberal that wants to live in a novelty world where everyone hugs everyone and there's nothing but pictures of cute little kittens instead of the reality of a world where others are out to rob, cheat and steal from you or countries and groups are out to commit complete genocide of your group if given the slightest chance. Now that's a dangerous genetic defect that the blinders can and have had dismal effects.

Liberals tend to blindly follow a leader that offers the dream of the novelty seeking individual, they do this without thought and without consequence to themselves or others. They do this to such a predictable format that every response to every argument presented to them with or without facts have a very predictable response over and over. The response never include facts and only make sense if you don't think about them.

Remember while not taught in most schools there is the fact that the democratic party did in fact create the KKK and its purpose was to suppress others that didn't think their way, even and usually to the point of killing them. The KKK original targets where republicans and they then targeted blacks that wouldn't promise not to vote for a republican.[cxlii]

Political liberalism is a deadly consequence of the defect and now that it has been identified as genetic defect it is important that we can come up with a fast reasonable solution for these subjects before they are permitted to devastate the world as we know it. A world led by liberalism would at the very least end evolution's direction from being stronger, smarter and better equipped to deal with real problems or at the worst and most predictable outcome humans would simply become extinct and disappear from the planet well before evolution could have a hand in anything.

The only positive outcome from these studies would be that we are aware of this genetic defect and can position ourselves to better handle those with the defect. Attempt to create a cure or treatment plan that can ID these individuals at a young enough age that they can have the tools to overcome the devastating effects of the genetic defect.

It Is Possible to Overcome

With all the gloom and doom of this one may think "let's just through in the towel" but that's not the answer and not the suggestion here. Like most all things with behavior, one can think of it as a muscle as well as learn from others.

It is known that generally humans seek out companions that have the same types of beliefs and moral standings as they do. Not always are all friends that way but generally speaking most of the friends and acquaintances will be that way. There are always other factors that bring in others from different circles of beliefs and moral standings.

It is also known that the mind and behaviors are both like muscles and the more you flex and feed them then the stronger and more desirable they become. Weight lifters spend most of their lives overcoming the skinny litter runt they once were and then spend a huge part of the life maintaining the desired results as do the people who have the ability to use their minds rapidly to make life threating decisions (Doctors, fighter pilots among just one group) spend a large part of their lives getting their brain to think correctly and then spend a lot of time maintaining that level.

Basically depending on how deeply rooted the genetic defect currently is will be the deciding factor as to how much work will be needed to overcome the genetic defects. No matter what the case may be the path will begin with the subject being entirely honest and if they aren't willing to do that then there is little chance of overcoming the defect.

Addicts of all kinds go through many different types of rehab and different medical treatments few are successful the first time due to them not truly wanting to overcome the effects of the defect. In the next chapter we will outline the basics that without these the subject is just setting themselves up for failure.

Living Productively with The Effects of The DRD4 Genetic Defects

Some will say things when they read this book that I am talking out my ass and some will actually look at what is being said and see that this is truly an answer that many have been looking for, for a long time. It's not my concern how you look at this or what you take from it, I am just putting this out there so that those who really want to change can and those who don't want to change could at least see the truth for the first time.

One good thing about the brain and the effects of the DRD4 genetic defect is that a lot of the effects seems to weaken after age 45. That's important and relevant to the following sections. Some things that we know about this is that at a certain age one actually has learned from the past enough to go through these steps without realizing it. The old adage that "If you're in college and a liberal, you will outgrow it" seems to hold some weight to it.

We spoke a lot about the genetic defects and the effects that they have on ones thinking as well as going into depth about not only how the behavior can be permitted to be deeply rooted but that there are possibilities of being able to overcome them and that there are certain types of structures that are built and strengthened by both negative as well as positive behaviors. By now you know more about the DRD4 genetic defects then most ever need to know so let's put some of the proven methods to use and see the results by overcoming the effects.

Remember the DRD4 gene is a link to dopamine and of course most of our brains love dopamine and those with the DRD4 genetic defect have a hard time living without huge amounts of it. This causes the brain to cause all kinds of issues when it is aware of the possibility of not getting the surge, the brain can cause real feelings of pain, depression, paranoia and alternate realities. That's why it's important for the subject to know the facts and want to truly overcome the effects.

This is no easy process for the person and they must be dedicated or they are simply setting themselves up for failure. Speaking in the addict world it is common for the addict to always hold close as a lifesaving resource their supplier and methods to find new ones.

Our Circles

As stated earlier on human tend to gather in familiar circles, creating a safer place for them to blend in and not challenge their beliefs, a circle that is comfortable as well as a circle that is nurturing to the brains perception of what it thinks is best for them.

Many rehabs and support groups will state at the very beginning that in order to overcome you must create a new circle of friends and eliminate completely all of them that don't have the same beliefs and values as you are trying to get to.

This means blocking numbers of those people, deleting them from you contacts and not seeking out others that may provide you with the negatives that you are trying so hard to get rid of. This seems easy however I know for a fact that it's not and the more one thinks about it the harder it is for them.

It's one of the most important steps as well as the hardest and must be followed. We've built a life around these circles so it's not going to be easy by any means but it is totally possible. One must not permit themselves to continue to even have access to the old circle.

Start finding a new circle by going to places where the desired people you want in the new circle are, locating the people at work that may be in the desired new circle already and bring them into your new circle. Support groups have positives but remember anyone who had the same issues you have already belong to the old circle and do not make a good first choice for a new circle.

Thinking and Muscles

This too is a major step, as we have spent most of our lives building the negative methods for coping and even general thought patterns. We've flexed that muscle so much that it has become massive and has no problems with taking over if given the slightest chance.

This step is after eliminating the old circle of friends for a reason. As long as the old friends and that circle exist then they will add to the muscle of the old thought patterns and will, even if unknowingly make life very difficult for any progress. That circle and those friends must remain out of reach.

Your new goals must remain top priority and new habits must be reinforced. Stop looking at others who have lived with the same issues their entire lives without issues as role models and start looking for roles models that have qualities that would draw people in general to them as your first qualifier and the one that holds the most weight.

Write down what you think someone without the issues you are trying to overcome might have for goals, routines and even the general outlook of these people. They will change over time as you get closer to that goal and that's fine, it shows growth in the right direction.

Write down your current goals and routines and then replace the negative ones in that list with the positive list. Practice the routines, try time out whether it be going to the gym, walking by the river or sporting events or even getting up at the same time everyday no matter what, having breakfast maybe just getting up and going for a quick walk. The goal here is to create a few positive routines that can get rooted into you mind. Look at your goals and cross out the negative ones (Scoring a fix, convincing someone that your different now) and put in a few positive ones or even focus on any positive ones you currently have but here we want to eliminate the ones that are negative.

Remember as an addict you are extremely capable of being very manipulative, what you don't know is just how much your brain is capable of being manipulative to you. Guaranteed that your brain is at least ten times better at manipulating you then you are of someone else. Your brain can and will make you feel pain, be sick and even have an altered sense of reality in order to get the dopamine that it wants.

You will get better with time with these because as you continue you will be building the new muscle while letting the other muscle slowly disappear.

There are no quick fixes here only a path that must be taken in order to reach happiness without the negative behavior that once controlled your life. Remember this is a guide that takes work and work like you have never before faced. You will face hurdles and will have that old muscle trying to slap you around every chance it gets, however remember it is possible, others have done it and you can too.

Giving Up Old Behavior

Here is what some see as the hardest part for an addict and depending what the addiction is will depend on the different levels of difficulties one will face. Some addictions have both chemical as well as psychological addictions and each must be overcome for the desired results, both are difficult and it is hard to tell when one stops and the other takes over. For the outcome to work you must replace the negative thoughts with positive, it's been proven that even in die hard heroin addicts that the psychological addiction is a lot worse than the chemical addiction.

My belief is that you bust give up what your addicted to completely. For instance I can't say I quit smoking because I switched brands, I can't say I'm not addicted to sex anymore because I know only have sex with same sex partners and I can't say I gave up heroin when I'm taking methadone. Why not you say? Well sex is sex and while it's psychological addiction to the actual cigarette it's a chemical addiction to nicotine and while its psychological addiction to heroin it's a chemical addiction to opiates and in those cases we never stopped the addiction.

Now I've been called wrong and there are studies about methadone that states that it has been successful as a maintenance for heroin and as a maintenance I could accept, it's cheaper, it's safer and its legal. Almost every methadone clinic's website or brochure uses the reference that society lets a person with asthma use an inhaler and since addiction is a disease then heroin addicts can take methadone the same way and that society needs to change their way of thinking, that would work well if the restaurant that I go to would stop classifying my Marlboro's as cigarettes when we all know that Winston's are cigarettes.

I've also have never seen a methadone clinic that acted like anything else besides a legal drug dealer, they tend to promote and get addicts on a larger dose because they know that methadone is a lot harder to come off of then heroin so just like the dealer giving away free samples to get you hooked they are doing their best to make sure your primary goal in life is getting to the clinic before they close and coming up with the dosing fee at any moral cost available and without regard of the patient.

I'm not trying to bash the methadone clinic and think that if they was to change their promotions to be accurate then there wouldn't be as much of a problem with them. I tried real hard to find one example of someone that successfully used methadone to get off of opiates and I was unsuccessful in finding even one example, I even called 25 different clinics posing as a heroin addict and they all were extremely careful to not say that I would ever have a chance to get off of opiates and instead referred to a maintenance program of an opiate as there first choice.

So with those that choose not to give up opiates and go the same way as the sex addict below I recommend looking at the negative attributes of the opiate addiction and look at giving up them. They are the same for the most part as the sex addict so I will type them below.

With sex it is hard due to the psychological effects and because no one totally gives up sex unless you're a nun its much like the methadone method. So while you might not give up sex you need to look at the other things within the addiction that are negatives and focus on them as well.

For both sex addicts and opiate addicts where neither are intending on giving them up totally this will help. First be sure to dealing with the previous two steps they are very important to any addictions. Secondly take an extra look at the "Thinking and Muscle" section and add into your goals and thinking patterns to install a strong sense of moral values, values that will keep you from lying, cheating and stealing and push real hard to make these your primary goal every morning when you wake up. Look at yourself in the mirror before bed and ask if you've made it a day with those morals intact and repeat every day.

If sex and opiate addicts take that advice then they will minimize the hurt they cause to others as well as to themselves. So it can't be stressed enough.

Now for liberals, this is a bit different because there are liberals that aren't effected by the genetic defect, grant it few of them. Some of the traits that must be looked at and focused on is the moral concepts as well as looking at what you can do for others without getting a reward for in one way or another.

Not all liberals are bad so you have to evaluate why you are a liberal and if any reasons that come out of your mouth is a canned result then you've not read this. I would suggest starting over and continue until you can answer the question.

Once you've been able to answer it then you can start

looking at the negative parts of it (yes that any part where you profit in any way with any rewards at all) and focus on those attributes to improve on.

I'm not saying you need to become a conservative in any way, I am saying that you need to know what you are and why you are and eliminate the negatives and increase the positives.

These steps will help all overcome the negative effects of the DRD4 genetic defects, they will make you a better person that you can truly respect and that others will be inspired by. They will make you a happier person for the right reasons and a contributing member of society.

ABOUT THE AUTHOR

I am Terry, I have 20 + years in technology including VoIP, Networking and Software design. I owned a technology company for 18 years working with large hospitals, government agencies, businesses and the general population.

I generally tell things like they are while using plain language. I feel that if the words have to be steam cleaned and pressed to be on pages then they aren't worth reading.

Enjoy the books and the different style of writing. There are more to come.

The DRD4 genetic defect controls may different personality traits as well as believes that seem to be coming from ones core.

This doesn't need to be a bad thing and the good news is that many function in society without the DRD4 ever getting in the way, some struggle many years and some will never be productive on their own.

Here you could of understood why and possibly with that knowledge you could be able to be productive in society.

[i] Van Tol HH, Bunzow JR, Guan HC, Sunahara RK, Seeman P, Niznik HB, Civelli O (Apr 1991). "Cloning of the gene for a human dopamine D4 receptor with high affinity for the antipsychotic clozapine". Nature 350 (6319): 610–4. doi:10.1038/350610a0. PMID 1840645.

[ii] Ptácek R, Kuzelová H, Stefano GB (Sep 2011). "Dopamine D4 receptor gene DRD4 and its association with psychiatric disorders". Medical Science Monitor 17 (9): RA215–RA220. doi:10.12659/MSM.881925. PMC 3560519. PMID 21873960.

[iii] Domschke K (Jul 2013). "Clinical and molecular genetics of psychotic depression". Schizophrenia Bulletin 39 (4): 766–75. doi:10.1093/schbul/sbt040. PMID 23512949.

[iv] McGeary J (Sep 2009). "The DRD4 exon 3 VNTR polymorphism and addiction-related phenotypes: a review". Pharmacology, Biochemistry, and Behavior 93 (3): 222–9. doi:10.1016/j.pbb.2009.03.010. PMID 19336242.

[v] Cormier F, Muellner J, Corvol JC (Apr 2013). "Genetics of impulse control disorders in Parkinson's disease". Journal of Neural Transmission 120 (4): 665–71. doi:10.1007/s00702-012-0934-4. PMID 23232665.

[vi] Rask-Andersen M, Olszewski PK, Levine AS, Schiöth HB (Mar 2010). "Molecular mechanisms underlying anorexia nervosa: focus on human gene association studies and systems controlling food intake". Brain Research Reviews 62 (2): 147–64. doi:10.1016/j.brainresrev.2009.10.007.

PMID 19931559.

[vii] Ptáček R, Kuželová H, Stefano GB, Raboch J, Kream RM (Apr 2013). "Targeted D4 dopamine receptors: implications for drug discovery and therapeutic development". Current Drug Targets 14 (4): 507–12. doi:10.2174/1389450111314040012. PMID 23469923.

[viii] Neve KA, Seamans JK, Trantham-Davidson H (Aug 2004). "Dopamine receptor signaling". Journal of Receptor and Signal Transduction Research 24 (3): 165–205. doi:10.1081/RRS-200029981. PMID 15521361.

[ix] Catalano M, Nobile M, Novelli E, Nöthen MM, Smeraldi E (Oct 1993). "Distribution of a novel mutation in the first exon of the human dopamine D4 receptor gene in psychotic patients". Biological Psychiatry 34 (7): 459–64. doi:10.1016/0006-3223(93)90236-7. PMID 8268330.

[x] Thapar A, Langley K, Owen MJ, O'Donovan MC (Dec 2007). "Advances in genetic findings on attention deficit hyperactivity disorder". Psychological Medicine 37 (12): 1681–92. doi:10.1017/S0033291707000773. PMID 17506925.

[xi] Gene Overview of All Published Schizophrenia-Association Studies for DRD4 - SzGene database at Schizophrenia Research Forum.

[xii] Munafò MR, Yalcin B, Willis-Owen SA, Flint J (Jan 2008). "Association of the dopamine D4 receptor (DRD4) gene and approach-related personality traits: meta-analysis

and new data". Biological Psychiatry 63 (2): 197–206. doi:10.1016/j.biopsych.2007.04.006. PMID 17574217.

[xiii] Wu J, Xiao H, Sun H, Zou L, Zhu LQ (Jun 2012). "Role of dopamine receptors in ADHD: a systematic meta-analysis". Molecular Neurobiology 45 (3): 605–20. doi:10.1007/s12035-012-8278-5. PMID 22610946.

[xiv] Faraone SV, Doyle AE, Mick E, Biederman J (Jul 2001). "Meta-analysis of the association between the 7-repeat allele of the dopamine D(4) receptor gene and attention deficit hyperactivity disorder". The American Journal of Psychiatry 158 (7): 1052–7. doi:10.1176/appi.ajp.158.7.1052. PMID 11431226.

[xv] Wang E, Ding YC, Flodman P, Kidd JR, Kidd KK, Grady DL, Ryder OA, Spence MA, Swanson JM, Moyzis RK (May 2004). "The genetic architecture of selection at the human dopamine receptor D4 (DRD4) gene locus". American Journal of Human Genetics 74 (5): 931–44. doi:10.1086/420854. PMC 1181986. PMID 15077199.

[xvi] Asghari V, Sanyal S, Buchwaldt S, Paterson A, Jovanovic V, Van Tol HH (Sep 1995). "Modulation of intracellular cyclic AMP levels by different human dopamine D4 receptor variants". Journal of Neurochemistry 65 (3): 1157–1165. doi:10.1046/j.1471-4159.1995.65031157.x. PMID 7643093.

[xvii] Wang E, Ding YC, Flodman P, Kidd JR, Kidd KK, Grady DL, Ryder OA, Spence MA, Swanson JM, Moyzis RK (May 2004). "The genetic architecture of selection at the human dopamine receptor D4 (DRD4) gene locus".

American Journal of Human Genetics 74 (5): 931–44. doi:10.1086/420854. PMC 1181986. PMID 15077199.

[xviii] Chen CS, Burton M, Greenberger E, Dmitrieva J (September 1999). "Population migration and the variation of dopamine D4 receptor (DRD4) allele frequencies around the globe". Evolution and Human Behavior 20 (5): 309–324. doi:10.1016/S1090-5138(99)00015-X.

[xix] Eisenberg DT, Campbell B, Gray PB, Sorenson MD (2008). "Dopamine receptor genetic polymorphisms and body composition in undernourished pastoralists: an exploration of nutrition indices among nomadic and recently settled Ariaal men of northern Kenya". BMC Evolutionary Biology 8: 173. doi:10.1186/1471-2148-8-173. PMC 2440754. PMID 18544160.

[xx] Munafò MR, Yalcin B, Willis-Owen SA, Flint J (Jan 2008). "Association of the dopamine D4 receptor (DRD4) gene and approach-related personality traits: meta-analysis and new data". Biological Psychiatry 63 (2): 197–206. doi:10.1016/j.biopsych.2007.04.006. PMID 17574217.

[xxi] Posner MI, Rothbart MK, Sheese BE, Voelker P (May 2012). "Control networks and neuromodulators of early development". Developmental Psychology 48 (3): 827–35. doi:10.1037/a0025530. PMID 21942663.

[xxii] Posner MI, Rothbart MK, Sheese BE, Voelker P (May 2012). "Control networks and neuromodulators of early development". Developmental Psychology 48 (3): 827–35. doi:10.1037/a0025530. PMID 21942663.

[xxiii] Posner MI, Rothbart MK, Sheese BE, Voelker P (May 2012). "Control networks and neuromodulators of early development". Developmental Psychology 48 (3): 827–35. doi:10.1037/a0025530. PMID 21942663.

[xxiv] Posner MI, Rothbart MK, Sheese BE, Voelker P (May 2012). "Control networks and neuromodulators of early development". Developmental Psychology 48 (3): 827–35. doi:10.1037/a0025530. PMID 21942663.

[xxv] Chemel BR, Roth BL, Armbruster B, Watts VJ, Nichols DE (Oct 2006). "WAY-100635 is a potent dopamine D4 receptor agonist". Psychopharmacology 188 (2): 244–51. doi:10.1007/s00213-006-0490-4. PMID 16915381.

[xxvi] Moreland RB, Patel M, Hsieh GC, Wetter JM, Marsh K, Brioni JD (Sep 2005). "A-412997 is a selective dopamine D4 receptor agonist in rats". Pharmacology, Biochemistry, and Behavior 82 (1): 140–7. doi:10.1016/j.pbb.2005.08.001. PMID 16153699.

[xxvii] Cowart M, Latshaw SP, Bhatia P, Daanen JF, Rohde J, Nelson SL, Patel M, Kolasa T, Nakane M, Uchic ME, Miller LN, Terranova MA, Chang R, Donnelly-Roberts DL, Namovic MT, Hollingsworth PR, Martino BR, Lynch JJ, Sullivan JP, Hsieh GC, Moreland RB, Brioni JD, Stewart AO (Jul 2004). "Discovery of 2-(4-pyridin-2-ylpiperazin-1-ylmethyl)-1H-benzimidazole (ABT-724), a dopaminergic agent with a novel mode of action for the potential treatment of erectile dysfunction". Journal of Medicinal Chemistry 47 (15): 3853–64. doi:10.1021/jm030505a. PMID 15239663.

[xxviii] Patel MV, Kolasa T, Mortell K, Matulenko MA, Hakeem

AA, Rohde JJ, Nelson SL, Cowart MD, Nakane M, Miller LN, Uchic ME, Terranova MA, El-Kouhen OF, Donnelly-Roberts DL, Namovic MT, Hollingsworth PR, Chang R, Martino BR, Wetter JM, Marsh KC, Martin R, Darbyshire JF, Gintant G, Hsieh GC, Moreland RB, Sullivan JP, Brioni JD, Stewart AO (Dec 2006). "Discovery of 3-methyl-N-(1-oxy-3',4',5',6'-tetrahydro-2'H-[2,4'-bipyridine]-1'-ylmethyl)benzamide (ABT-670), an orally bioavailable dopamine D4 agonist for the treatment of erectile dysfunction". Journal of Medicinal Chemistry 49 (25): 7450–65. doi:10.1021/jm060662k. PMID 17149874.

[xxix] Hübner H, Kraxner J, Gmeiner P (Nov 2000). "Cyanoindole derivatives as highly selective dopamine D(4) receptor partial agonists: solid-phase synthesis, binding assays, and functional experiments". Journal of Medicinal Chemistry 43 (23): 4563–9. doi:10.1021/jm0009989. PMID 11087581.

[xxx] Hübner H, Kraxner J, Gmeiner P (Nov 2000). "Cyanoindole derivatives as highly selective dopamine D(4) receptor partial agonists: solid-phase synthesis, binding assays, and functional experiments". Journal of Medicinal Chemistry 43 (23): 4563–9. doi:10.1021/jm0009989. PMID 11087581.

[xxxi] Kolasa T, Matulenko MA, Hakeem AA, Patel MV, Mortell K, Bhatia P, Henry R, Nakane M, Hsieh GC, Terranova MA, Uchic ME, Miller LN, Chang R, Donnelly-Roberts DL, Namovic MT, Hollingsworth PR, Martino B, El Kouhen O, Marsh KC, Wetter JM, Moreland RB, Brioni JD, Stewart AO (Aug 2006). "1-aryl-3-(4-pyridine-2-

ylpiperazin-1-yl)propan-1-one oximes as potent dopamine D4 receptor agonists for the treatment of erectile dysfunction". Journal of Medicinal Chemistry 49 (17): 5093–109. doi:10.1021/jm060279f. PMID 16913699.

[xxxii] Enguehard-Gueiffier C, Hübner H, El Hakmaoui A, Allouchi H, Gmeiner P, Argiolas A, Melis MR, Gueiffier A (Jun 2006). "2-[(4-phenylpiperazin-1-yl)methyl]imidazo(di)azines as selective D4-ligands. Induction of penile erection by 2-[4-(2-methoxyphenyl)piperazin-1-ylmethyl]imidazo[1,2-a]pyridine (PIP3EA), a potent and selective D4 partial agonist". Journal of Medicinal Chemistry 49 (13): 3938–47. doi:10.1021/jm060166w. PMID 16789750.

[xxxiii] Nakane M, Cowart MD, Hsieh GC, Miller L, Uchic ME, Chang R, Terranova MA, Donnelly-Roberts DL, Namovic MT, Miller TR, Wetter JM, Marsh K, Stewart AO, Brioni JD, Moreland RB (Jul 2005). "2-[4-(3,4-Dimethylphenyl)piperazin-1-ylmethyl]-1H benzoimidazole (A-381393), a selective dopamine D4 receptor antagonist". Neuropharmacology 49 (1): 112–21. doi:10.1016/j.neuropharm.2005.02.004. PMID 15992586.

[xxxiv] Prante O, Tietze R, Hocke C, Löber S, Hübner H, Kuwert T, Gmeiner P (Mar 2008). "Synthesis, radiofluorination, and in vitro evaluation of pyrazolo[1,5-a]pyridine-based dopamine D4 receptor ligands: discovery of an inverse agonist radioligand for PET". Journal of Medicinal Chemistry 51 (6): 1800–10. doi:10.1021/jm701375u. PMID 18307287.

[xxxv] Kulagowski JJ, Broughton HB, Curtis NR, Mawer IM, Ridgill MP, Baker R, Emms F, Freedman SB, Marwood R,

Patel S, Patel S, Ragan CI, Leeson PD (May 1996). "3-((4-(4-Chlorophenyl)piperazin-1-yl)-methyl)-1H-pyrrolo-2,3-b-pyridine: an antagonist with high affinity and selectivity for the human dopamine D4 receptor". Journal of Medicinal Chemistry 39 (10): 1941–2. doi:10.1021/jm9600712. PMID 8642550.

[xxxvi] Kulagowski JJ, Broughton HB, Curtis NR, Mawer IM, Ridgill MP, Baker R, Emms F, Freedman SB, Marwood R, Patel S, Patel S, Ragan CI, Leeson PD (May 1996). "3-((4-(4-Chlorophenyl)piperazin-1-yl)-methyl)-1H-pyrrolo-2,3-b-pyridine: an antagonist with high affinity and selectivity for the human dopamine D4 receptor". Journal of Medicinal Chemistry 39 (10): 1941–2. doi:10.1021/jm9600712. PMID 8642550.

[xxxvii] Patel S, Freedman S, Chapman KL, Emms F, Fletcher AE, Knowles M, Marwood R, Mcallister G, Myers J, Curtis N, Kulagowski JJ, Leeson PD, Ridgill M, Graham M, Matheson S, Rathbone D, Watt AP, Bristow LJ, Rupniak NM, Baskin E, Lynch JJ, Ragan CI (Nov 1997). "Biological profile of L-745,870, a selective antagonist with high affinity for the dopamine D4 receptor". The Journal of Pharmacology and Experimental Therapeutics 283 (2): 636–47. PMID 9353380.

[xxxviii] Millan MJ, Newman-Tancredi A, Brocco M, Gobert A, Lejeune F, Audinot V, Rivet JM, Schreiber R, Dekeyne A, Spedding M, Nicolas JP, Peglion JL (Oct 1998). "S 18126 ([2-[4-(2,3-dihydrobenzo[1,4]dioxin-6-yl)piperazin-1-yl methyl]indan-2-yl]), a potent, selective and competitive antagonist at dopamine D4 receptors: an in vitro and in vivo comparison with L 745,870 (3-(4-[4-chlorophenyl]piperazin-1-yl)methyl-1H-pyrrolo[2,

3b]pyridine) and raclopride". The Journal of
Pharmacology and Experimental Therapeutics 287 (1):
167–86. PMID 9765336.

3b]pyridine) and raclopride". The Journal of
Pharmacology and Experimental Therapeutics 287 (1):
167–86. PMID 9765336.

[xxxix] Kulagowski JJ, Broughton HB, Curtis NR, Mawer IM,
Ridgill MP, Baker R, Emms F, Freedman SB, Marwood R,
Patel S, Patel S, Ragan CI, Leeson PD (May 1996). "3-((4-
(4-Chlorophenyl)piperazin-1-yl)-methyl)-1H-pyrrolo-2,3-b-
pyridine: an antagonist with high affinity and selectivity
for the human dopamine D4 receptor". Journal of
Medicinal Chemistry 39 (10): 1941–2.
doi:10.1021/jm9600712. PMID 8642550.

[xl] Lanig H, Utz W, Gmeiner P (Apr 2001). "Comparative
molecular field analysis of dopamine D4 receptor
antagonists including 3-[4-(4-chlorophenyl) piperazin-1-
ylmethyl] pyrazolo[1,5-a]pyridine (FAUC 113), 3-[4-(4-
chlorophenyl)piperazin-1-ylmethyl]-1H-pyrrolo-[2,3-
b]pyridine (L-745,870), and clozapine". Journal of
Medicinal Chemistry 44 (8): 1151–7.
doi:10.1021/jm001055e. PMID 11312915.

[xli] Ebstein RP. Saga of an adventure gene: novelty seeking,
substance abuse and the dopamine D4 receptor exon III
repeat polymorphism. Mol Psychiatry 1997; 2: 381,384,

[xlii] Baron M. Mapping genes in personality: is the saga
sagging? Mol Psychiatry 1998; 3: 106,108,

[xliii] Lusher J, Ebersole L, Ball D. Dopamine D4 receptor
gene and severity of dependence. Addict Biol 2000; 5:
471,474,

[xliv] Ebstein RP, Novick O, Umansky R, Priel B, Osher Y,

Blaine D et al. Dopamine D4 receptor (DRD4) exon III polymorphism associated with the human personality trait of novelty seeking. Nature Genet 1996; 12: 78,80, MEDLINE

[xlv] Cloninger CR. Tridimensional Personality Questionnaire Version 4. Washington University Press: St Louis, 1987,

[xlvi] Benjamin J, Li L, Patterson C, Greenberg BD, Murphy DL, Hamer DH. Population and familial association between the D4 dopamine receptor gene and measures of novelty seeking. Nature Genet 1996; 12: 81,84, MEDLINE

[xlvii] Ebstein RP, Novick O, Umansky R, Priel B, Osher Y, Blaine D et al. Dopamine D4 receptor (DRD4) exon III polymorphism associated with the human personality trait of novelty seeking. Nature Genet 1996; 12: 78,80, MEDLINE

[xlviii] Ebstein RP. Saga of an adventure gene: novelty seeking, substance abuse and the dopamine D4 receptor exon III repeat polymorphism. Mol Psychiatry 1997; 2: 381,384,

[xlix] Ebstein RP. Saga of an adventure gene: novelty seeking, substance abuse and the dopamine D4 receptor exon III repeat polymorphism. Mol Psychiatry 1997; 2: 381,384,

[l] Ono Y, Manki H, Yoshimura K et al. Association between dopamine D4 receptor exon II polymorphism and novelty seeking in Japanese subjects. Am J Med Genet 1997; 74: 501,503,

[li] Noble EP, Ozkaragoz T, Ritchie TL, Zhang X, Belin TR, Sparkes RS. D2 and D4 dopamine receptor polymorphisms and personality. Am J Med Genet 1998; 81: 257,267,

[lii] Ekelund J, Lichtermann D, Jarvelin MR, Peltonen L. Association between novelty seeking and the type 4 dopamine receptor gene in a large Finnish cohort sample. Am J Psychiatry 1999; 156: 1453,1455, MEDLINE

[liii] Tomitaka M, Tomitaka SI, Otuka Y, Kim K, Matuki H, Sakamoto K et al. Association between novelty seeking and dopamine receptor D4 exon III polymorphism in Japanese subjects. Am J Med Genet 1999; 88: 469,471,

[liv] Strobel A, Wehr A, Michel A, Brocke B. Association between the dopamine D4 receptor (DRD4) exon III polymorphism and measures of novelty seeking in a German population. Mol Psychiatry 1999; 4: 378,384, MEDLINE

[lv] Okuyama Y, Ishiguro H, Nankai M, Shibuya H, Watanabe A, Arinami T. Identification of a polymorphism in the promoter region of DRD4 associated with the human novelty seeking personality trait. Mol Psychiatry 2000; 5: 64,69, MEDLINE

[lvi] Benjamin J, Osher Y, Kotler M, Gritsenko I, Nemanov L, Belmaker RH et al. Association between tridimensional personality questionnaire (TPQ) traits and three functional polymorphisms: dopamine receptor D4 (DRD4), serotonin transporter promoter region (5-HTTLPR) and catechol O-methyltransferase (COMT). Mol Psychiatry

2000; 5: 96,100, MEDLINE

[lvii] Noble EP, Ozkaragoz T, Ritchie TL, Zhang X, Belin TR, Sparkes RS. D2 and D4 dopamine receptor polymorphisms and personality. Am J Med Genet 1998; 81: 257,267,

[lviii] Ekelund J, Lichtermann D, Jarvelin MR, Peltonen L. Association between novelty seeking and the type 4 dopamine receptor gene in a large Finnish cohort sample. Am J Psychiatry 1999; 156: 1453,1455, MEDLINE

[lix] Benjamin J, Osher Y, Kotler M, Gritsenko I, Nemanov L, Belmaker RH et al. Association between tridimensional personality questionnaire (TPQ) traits and three functional polymorphisms: dopamine receptor D4 (DRD4), serotonin transporter promoter region (5-HTTLPR) and catechol O-methyltransfarese (COMT). Mol Psychiatry 2000; 5: 96,100, MEDLINE

[lx] Strobel A, Wehr A, Michel A, Brocke B. Association between the dopamine D4 receptor (DRD4) exon III polymorphism and measures of novelty seeking in a German population. Mol Psychiatry 1999; 4: 378,384, MEDLINE

[lxi] Malhotra AK, Virkkunen M, Rooney W, Eggert M, Linnoila M, Goldman D. The association between dopamine (D4DR) 16 amino acid repeat and novelty seeking. Mol Psychiatry 1996; 1: 388,391,

[lxii] Pogue-Geile M, Deka R, Debski T, Manuck S. Human novelty-seeking personality traits and dopamine D4 receptor polymorphisms: a twin and genetic association

study. Am J Med Genet 1998; 81: 44,48,

[lxiii] Benjamin J, Osher Y, Belmaker RH, Ebstein RP. No significant associations between two dopamine receptor polymorphisms and normal temperament. Hum Psychopharmacol 1998; 13: 11,15,

[lxiv] Jonsson EG, Nothen MM, Gustavsson JP, Neidt H, Forslund K, Evenden M et al. Lack of association between dopamine D4 receptor gene and personality traits. Psychol Med 1998; 28: 985,989, Article MEDLINE

[lxv] Gelernter J, Kranzler H, Coccaro E, Siever L, New A, Mulgrew CL. D4 dopamine-receptor (DRD4) alleles and novelty seeking in substance dependent, personality disorder and control subjects. Am J Hum Genet 1997; 61: 1144,1152,

[lxvi] Jonsson EG, Nothen MM, Gustavsson JP, Neidt H, Brene S, Tylec A et al. Lack of evidence for allelic association between personality traits and the dopamine D4 receptor gene polymorphisms. Am J Psychiatry 1997; 154: 697,699, MEDLINE

[lxvii] Vandebergh DJ, Zonderman AB, Wang J, Uhl GR, Costa PT. No association between novelty seeking and dopamine receptor (D4DR) exon III seven repeat alleles in Baltimore longitudinal study of ageing participants. Mol Psychiatry 1997; 2: 417,419,

[lxviii] Kuhn K, Meyer K, Nothen M, Gansicke M, Papassotiropoulos A, Maier W. Allelic variants of dopamine receptor D4 and serotonin receptor 5HT2c and temperatment factors: replication tests. Am J Med Genet

1999; 88: 168,172,

[lxix] Bau CHD, Roman T, Almeida S, Hutz MH. Dopamine D4 receptor gene and personality dimensions in Brazilian male alcoholics. Psychiatr Genet 1999; 9: 139,143,

[lxx] Sullivan PF, Fifield WJ, Kennedy MA, Mulder RT, Sellman JD, Joyce PR. No association between novelty seeking and the type 4 dopamine receptor gene (DRD4) in two New Zealand samples. Am J Psychiatry 1997; 155: 98,101,

[lxxi] Ebstein RP. Saga of an adventure gene: novelty seeking, substance abuse and the dopamine D4 receptor exon III repeat polymorphism. Mol Psychiatry 1997; 2: 381,384,

[lxxii] Baron M. Mapping genes in personality: is the saga sagging? Mol Psychiatry 1998; 3: 106,108,

[lxxiii] Malhotra AK, Virkkunen M, Rooney W, Eggert M, Linnoila M, Goldman D. The association between dopamine (D4DR) 16 amino acid repeat and novelty seeking. Mol Psychiatry 1996; 1: 388,391,

[lxxiv] Gelernter J, Kranzler H, Coccaro E, Siever L, New A, Mulgrew CL. D4 dopamine-receptor (DRD4) alleles and novelty seeking in substance dependent, personality disorder and control subjects. Am J Hum Genet 1997; 61: 1144,1152,

[lxxv] Jonsson EG, Nothen MM, Gustavsson JP, Neidt H, Brene S, Tylec A et al. Lack of evidence for allelic association between personality traits and the dopamine D4 receptor gene polymorphisms. Am J Psychiatry 1997;

154: 697,699, MEDLINE

[lxxvi] Vandebergh DJ, Zonderman AB, Wang J, Uhl GR, Costa PT. No association between novelty seeking and dopamine receptor (D4DR) exon III seven repeat alleles in Baltimore longitudinal study of ageing participants. Mol Psychiatry 1997; 2: 417,419,

[lxxvii] Pogue-Geile M, Deka R, Debski T, Manuck S. Human novelty-seeking personality traits and dopamine D4 receptor polymorphisms: a twin and genetic association study. Am J Med Genet 1998; 81: 44,48,

[lxxviii] Benjamin J, Osher Y, Belmaker RH, Ebstein RP. No significant associations between two dopamine receptor polymorphisms and normal temperament. Hum Psychopharmacol 1998; 13: 11,15,

[lxxix] Jonsson EG, Nothen MM, Gustavsson JP, Neidt H, Forslund K, Evenden M et al. Lack of association between dopamine D4 receptor gene and personality traits. Psychol Med 1998; 28: 985,989, Article MEDLINE

[lxxx] Bau CHD, Roman T, Almeida S, Hutz MH. Dopamine D4 receptor gene and personality dimensions in Brazilian male alcoholics. Psychiatr Genet 1999; 9: 139,143,

[lxxxi] Kuhn K, Meyer K, Nothen M, Gansicke M, Papassotiropoulos A, Maier W. Allelic variants of dopamine receptor D4 and serotonin receptor 5HT2c and temperatment factors: replication tests. Am J Med Genet 1999; 88: 168,172,

lxxxii Bau CHD, Roman T, Almeida S, Hutz MH. Dopamine D4 receptor gene and personality dimensions in Brazilian male alcoholics. Psychiatr Genet 1999; 9: 139,143,

lxxxiii Zuckerman M. Sensation Seeking: Beyond the Optimal Level of Arousal. Lawrence Erlbaum: NJ,

lxxxiv Ebstein RP. Saga of an adventure gene: novelty seeking, substance abuse and the dopamine D4 receptor exon III repeat polymorphism. Mol Psychiatry 1997; 2: 381,384,

lxxxv Ebstein RP, Novick O, Umansky R, Priel B, Osher Y, Blaine D et al. Dopamine D4 receptor (DRD4) exon III polymorphism associated with the human personality trait of novelty seeking. Nature Genet 1996; 12: 78,80, MEDLINE

lxxxvi Benjamin J, Li L, Patterson C, Greenberg BD, Murphy DL, Hamer DH. Population and familial association between the D4 dopamine receptor gene and measures of novelty seeking. Nature Genet 1996; 12: 81,84, MEDLINE

lxxxvii Ono Y, Manki H, Yoshimura K et al. Association between dopamine D4 receptor exon II polymorphism and novelty seeking in Japanese subjects. Am J Med Genet 1997; 74: 501,503,

lxxxviii Noble EP, Ozkaragoz T, Ritchie TL, Zhang X, Belin TR, Sparkes RS. D2 and D4 dopamine receptor polymorphisms and personality. Am J Med Genet 1998; 81: 257,267,

lxxxix Ekelund J, Lichtermann D, Jarvelin MR, Peltonen L.

Association between novelty seeking and the type 4 dopamine receptor gene in a large Finnish cohort sample. Am J Psychiatry 1999; 156: 1453,1455, MEDLINE

[xc] Tomitaka M, Tomitaka SI, Otuka Y, Kim K, Matuki H, Sakamoto K et al. Association between novelty seeking and dopamine receptor D4 exon III polymorphism in Japanese subjects. Am J Med Genet 1999; 88: 469,471,

[xci] Strobel A, Wehr A, Michel A, Brocke B. Association between the dopamine D4 receptor (DRD4) exon III polymorphism and measures of novelty seeking in a German population. Mol Psychiatry 1999; 4: 378,384, MEDLINE

[xcii] Okuyama Y, Ishiguro H, Nankai M, Shibuya H, Watanabe A, Arinami T. Identification of a polymorphism in the promoter region of DRD4 associated with the human novelty seeking personality trait. Mol Psychiatry 2000; 5: 64,69, MEDLINE

[xciii] Benjamin J, Osher Y, Kotler M, Gritsenko I, Nemanov L, Belmaker RH et al. Association between tridimensional personality questionnaire (TPQ) traits and three functional polymorphisms: dopamine receptor D4 (DRD4), serotonin transporter promoter region (5-HTTLPR) and catechol O-methyltransferese (COMT). Mol Psychiatry 2000; 5: 96,100, MEDLINE

[xciv] Malhotra AK, Virkkunen M, Rooney W, Eggert M, Linnoila M, Goldman D. The association between dopamine (D4DR) 16 amino acid repeat and novelty

seeking. Mol Psychiatry 1996; 1: 388,391,

xcv Pogue-Geile M, Deka R, Debski T, Manuck S. Human novelty-seeking personality traits and dopamine D4 receptor polymorphisms: a twin and genetic association study. Am J Med Genet 1998; 81: 44,48,

xcvi Benjamin J, Osher Y, Belmaker RH, Ebstein RP. No significant associations between two dopamine receptor polymorphisms and normal temperament. Hum Psychopharmacol 1998; 13: 11,15,

xcvii Jonsson EG, Nothen MM, Gustavsson JP, Neidt H, Forslund K, Evenden M et al. Lack of association between dopamine D4 receptor gene and personality traits. Psychol Med 1998; 28: 985,989, Article MEDLINE

xcviii Gelernter J, Kranzler H, Coccaro E, Siever L, New A, Mulgrew CL. D4 dopamine-receptor (DRD4) alleles and novelty seeking in substance dependent, personality disorder and control subjects. Am J Hum Genet 1997; 61: 1144,1152,

xcix Jonsson EG, Nothen MM, Gustavsson JP, Neidt H, Brene S, Tylec A et al. Lack of evidence for allelic association between personality traits and the dopamine D4 receptor gene polymorphisms. Am J Psychiatry 1997; 154: 697,699, MEDLINE

c Vandebergh DJ, Zonderman AB, Wang J, Uhl GR, Costa PT. No association between novelty seeking and dopamine receptor (D4DR) exon III seven repeat alleles in Baltimore longitudinal study of ageing participants. Mol

Psychiatry 1997; 2: 417,419,

[ci] Kuhn K, Meyer K, Nothen M, Gansicke M, Papassotiropoulos A, Maier W. Allelic variants of dopamine receptor D4 and serotonin receptor 5HT2c and temperatment factors: replication tests. Am J Med Genet 1999; 88: 168,172,

[cii] Bau CHD, Roman T, Almeida S, Hutz MH. Dopamine D4 receptor gene and personality dimensions in Brazilian male alcoholics. Psychiatr Genet 1999; 9: 139,143,

[ciii] Sullivan PF, Fifield WJ, Kennedy MA, Mulder RT, Sellman JD, Joyce PR. No association between novelty seeking and the type 4 dopamine receptor gene (DRD4) in two New Zealand samples. Am J Psychiatry 1997; 155: 98,101,

[civ] Jonsson EG, Nothen MM, Gustavsson JP, Neidt H, Forslund K, Evenden M et al. Lack of association between dopamine D4 receptor gene and personality traits. Psychol Med 1998; 28: 985,989, Article MEDLINE

[cv] Gelernter J, Kranzler H, Coccaro E, Siever L, New A, Mulgrew CL. D4 dopamine-receptor (DRD4) alleles and novelty seeking in substance dependent, personality disorder and control subjects. Am J Hum Genet 1997; 61: 1144,1152,

[cvi] Jonsson EG, Nothen MM, Gustavsson JP, Neidt H, Brene S, Tylec A et al. Lack of evidence for allelic association between personality traits and the dopamine D4 receptor gene polymorphisms. Am J Psychiatry 1997; 154: 697,699, MEDLINE

[cvii] Vandebergh DJ, Zonderman AB, Wang J, Uhl GR, Costa PT. No association between novelty seeking and dopamine receptor (D4DR) exon III seven repeat alleles in Baltimore longitudinal study of ageing participants. Mol Psychiatry 1997; 2: 417,419,

[cviii] Bau CHD, Roman T, Almeida S, Hutz MH. Dopamine D4 receptor gene and personality dimensions in Brazilian male alcoholics. Psychiatr Genet 1999; 9: 139,143,

[cix] Sullivan PF, Fifield WJ, Kennedy MA, Mulder RT, Sellman JD, Joyce PR. No association between novelty seeking and the type 4 dopamine receptor gene (DRD4) in two New Zealand samples. Am J Psychiatry 1997; 155: 98,101,

[cx] Ebstein RP. Saga of an adventure gene: novelty seeking, substance abuse and the dopamine D4 receptor exon III repeat polymorphism. Mol Psychiatry 1997; 2: 381,384,

[cxi] Lusher J, Ebersole L, Ball D. Dopamine D4 receptor gene and severity of dependence. Addict Biol 2000; 5: 471,474,

[cxii] Ono Y, Manki H, Yoshimura K et al. Association between dopamine D4 receptor exon II polymorphism and novelty seeking in Japanese subjects. Am J Med Genet 1997; 74: 501,503,

[cxiii] Malhotra AK, Virkkunen M, Rooney W, Eggert M, Linnoila M, Goldman D. The association between dopamine (D4DR) 16 amino acid repeat and novelty seeking. Mol Psychiatry 1996; 1: 388,391,

[cxiv] Perez de Castro I, Ibanez A, Torres P, Saiz-Ruiz J,

Fernandez-Piqueras J. Genetic association study between pathological gambling and a functional DNA polymorphism at the D4 receptor gene. Pharmacogenetics 1997; 7: 345,348, MEDLINE

[cxv] Shields PG, Lerman C, Audrain J, Bowman ED, Main D, Boyd NR et al. Dopamine D4 receptors and the risk of cigarette smoking in African-Americans and Caucasians. Cancer, Epidemiol Biomark Prevent 1998; 7: 453,458,

[cxvi] Kotler M, Cohen H, Segman R, Gritsenko I, Nemanov L, Lerer B et al. Excess dopamine D4 receptor (DRD4) exon III seven repeat allele in opioid dependent subjects. Mol Psychiatry 1997; 2: 251,254, MEDLINE

[cxvii] Muramatsu T, Higuchi S, Murayama M, Matsushita S, Hayashida M. Association between alcoholism and the dopamine D receptor gene. J Med Genet 1996; 33: 113,115,

[cxviii] Li T, Xu K, Deng H, Cai G, Liu J, Liu X et al. Hypervariable segment in the dopamine receptor D4 gene. Hum Mol Genet 1993; 2: 767,773, MEDLINE

[cxix] Comings DE, Gonzalez N, Wu S, Gade R, Muhleman D, Saucier G et al. Studies of the 48 bp repeat polymorphism of the DRD4 gene in impulsive, compulsive, addictive behaviours. Am J Med Genet 1999; 88: 358,368, Article MEDLINE

[cxx] Sander T, Harms H, Dufeu P, Kuhn S. Dopamine D4 receptor exon III alleles and variation of novelty seeking in

alcoholics. Am J Med Genet 1997; 74: 483,487,

[cxxi] Roman T, Bau CHD, Almeida S, Hutz HM. Lack of association of the dopamine D4 receptor gene with alcoholism in a Brazilian population. Addict Biol 1999; 4: 203,207,

[cxxii] Franke P, Nothen MM, Wang T, Knapp M, Lichtermann D, Neidt H et al. DRD4 exon III VNTR polymorphism⊠susceptibility factor for heroin dependence? Results of a case-control and a family based association approach. Mol Psychiatry 2000; 5: 101,104, MEDLINE

[cxxiii] Ishiguro H, Saito T, Shibuya H, Arinami T. Association study between genetic polymorphisms the 14,3,3 chain and dopamine D4 receptor genes and alcoholism. Alcohol Clin Exp Res 2000; 24: 343,347,

[cxxiv] Parsian A, Chakraverty S, Fisher L, Cloninger CR. No association between polymorphisms in the human dopamine D3 and D4 receptors genes and alcoholism. Am J Med Genet 1997; 74: 281,285,

[cxxv] Geijer T, Jonsson E, Neiman J, Persson M, Brene S, Gyllander A et al. Tyrosine hydroxylase and dopamine D4 receptor allelic distribution in Scandinavian chronic alcoholics. J Clin Exp Res 1997; 21: 35,39,

[cxxvi] Chang FM, Kidd KK. Rapid molecular haplotyping of the first exon of the dopamine D4 receptor gene by heteroduplex analysis. Am J Med Genet 1997; 74: 91,94,

[cxxvii] Adamson MD, Kennedy J, Petronis A, Dean M, Virkkunen M, Linnoila M et al. DRD4 dopamine receptor genotype and CSF monoamine metabolites in Finnish alcoholics and controls. Am J Med Genet 1995; 60: 199,205,

[cxxviii] Shields PG, Lerman C, Audrain J, Bowman ED, Main D, Boyd NR et al. Dopamine D4 receptors and the risk of cigarette smoking in African-Americans and Caucasians. Cancer, Epidemiol Biomark Prevent 1998; 7: 453,458,

[cxxix] Kotler M, Cohen H, Segman R, Gritsenko I, Nemanov L, Lerer B et al. Excess dopamine D4 receptor (DRD4) exon III seven repeat allele in opioid dependent subjects. Mol Psychiatry 1997; 2: 251,254, MEDLINE

[cxxx] Li T, Xu K, Deng H, Cai G, Liu J, Liu X et al. Hypervariable segment in the dopamine receptor D4 gene. Hum Mol Genet 1993; 2: 767,773, MEDLINE

[cxxxi] Sander T, Harms H, Dufeu P, Kuhn S. Dopamine D4 receptor exon III alleles and variation of novelty seeking in alcoholics. Am J Med Genet 1997; 74: 483,487,

[cxxxii] Roman T, Bau CHD, Almeida S, Hutz HM. Lack of association of the dopamine D4 receptor gene with alcoholism in a Brazilian population. Addict Biol 1999; 4: 203,207,

[cxxxiii] Ishiguro H, Saito T, Shibuya H, Arinami T. Association study between genetic polymorphisms the 14,3,3 chain and dopamine D4 receptor genes and alcoholism. Alcohol Clin Exp Res 2000; 24: 343,347,

[cxxxiv] Parsian A, Chakraverty S, Fisher L, Cloninger CR. No association between polymorphisms in the human dopamine D3 and D4 receptors genes and alcoholism. Am J Med Genet 1997; 74: 281,285,

[cxxxv] Geijer T, Jonsson E, Neiman J, Persson M, Brene S, Gyllander A et al. Tyrosine hydroxylase and dopamine D4 receptor allelic distribution in Scandinavian chronic alcoholics. J Clin Exp Res 1997; 21: 35,39,

[cxxxvi] Chang FM, Kidd KK. Rapid molecular haplotyping of the first exon of the dopamine D4 receptor gene by heteroduplex analysis. Am J Med Genet 1997; 74: 91,94,

[cxxxvii] Adamson MD, Kennedy J, Petronis A, Dean M, Virkkunen M, Linnoila M et al. DRD4 dopamine receptor genotype and CSF monoamine metabolites in Finnish alcoholics and controls. Am J Med Genet 1995; 60: 199,205,

[cxxxviii] Muramatsu T, Higuchi S, Murayama M, Matsushita S, Hayashida M. Association between alcoholism and the dopamine D receptor gene. J Med Genet 1996; 33: 113,115,

[cxxxix] Lusher J, Ebersole L, Ball D. Dopamine D4 receptor gene and severity of dependence. Addict Biol 2000; 5: 471,474,

[cxl] Lusher J, Ebersole L, Ball D. Dopamine D4 receptor gene and severity of dependence. Addict Biol 2000; 5: 471,474,

[cxli] Ibanez A, Perez de Castro I, Fernandez-Piqueras J, Blanco C, Saiz-Ruiz J. Pathological gambling and DNA

polymorphic markers at MAO-A and MAO-B genes. Mol Psychiatry 2000; 5: 105,109, MEDLINE

[cxlii] David Barton of Wallbu More..ilders and published in his book "Setting the Record Straight: American History in Black & White," which reveals that not only did the Democrats work hand-in-glove with the Ku Klux Klan for generations, they started the KKK and endorsed its mayhem.